Headfirst Into Maths

Shape & Space

David Kirkby

Heinemann LIBRARY

First published in Great Britain by Heinemann Library,
Halley Court, Jordan Hill, Oxford OX2 8EJ,
a division of Reed Educational and Professional Publishing Ltd.
Heinemann is a registered trademark of Reed Educational & Professional Publishing Limited.

OXFORD MELBOURNE AUCKLAND
JOHANNESBURG BLANTYRE GABORONE
IBADAN PORTSMOUTH NH (USA) CHICAGO

Designed by Susan Clarke
Illustrations by Gillian Martin
Origination by Ambassador Litho Ltd
Printed by Wing King Tong in Hong Kong

03 02 01 00 99
10 9 8 7 6 5 4 3 2 1

ISBN 0 431 08019 4

British Library Cataloguing in Publication Data
Kirkby, David
Patterns. – (Head first into maths)
1.Geometry – Juvenile literature 2.Geometry – Problems,
exercises, etc. – Juvenile literature
I.Title
516.1'5

Acknowledgements
The Publishers would like to thank the following for permission to reproduce photographs:
Gareth Boden, p 28; J. Allen Cash, p. 22; Trevor Clifford, pp 4, 5, 8, 18, 20; Action Plus
Photographic (Glyn Kirk), p. 14.

Our thanks to Hilary Koll and Steve Mills for their comments in the preparation of this book.

Every effort has been made to contact copyright holders of any material reproduced
in this book. Any omissions will be rectified in subsequent printings if notice is given
to the Publisher.

For more information about Heinemann Library books, or to order, please phone 01865 888055,
or send a fax to 01865 314091. You can visit our web site at www.heinemann.co.uk

Contents

Any words appearing in the text in bold, **like this**, are explained in the Glossary

Flat shapes

Shapes which are flat, and drawn on a sheet of paper or card, are called shapes with two dimensions. They have length and width, but no thickness. Their length and width are their two dimensions. They are called **two-dimensional shapes**, or flat shapes.

For short, we sometimes say 2-D shape for two-dimensional shape.

◀ *These are not flat shapes, because the mats have thickness. The top of each mat is called its* **surface**. *Their surfaces are flat shapes.*

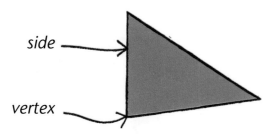

side

vertex

◀ *An* **edge** *of a flat shape is called a* **side**. *A corner is called a* **vertex**. *When you talk about more than one corner, you say* **vertices**.

4

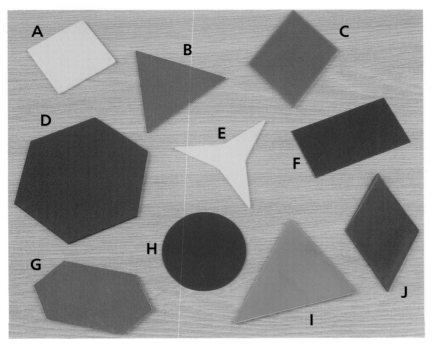

These shapes are not quite two-dimensional because they do have thickness, even though they are very thin. Their tops or surfaces, though, are flat shapes.

? Questions

How many sides does each shape have?

How many vertices does each have?

These are all two-dimensional shapes. They have no thickness.

Some shapes have sides which are straight, some have sides which are **curved**, and some have both straight and curved sides.

Use your head

How many shapes have sides that are:
all straight? all curved?
both straight and curved?

Fun to do

Draw your own set of different 2-D shapes on a large sheet of paper. Draw around objects to help you.

Angles

An **angle** is an amount of turn. When an object turns a small amount, it turns through a small angle; when it turns a large amount, it turns through a large angle.

▲ *The minute hand has turned a quarter-turn.*

◀ *The sail of the windmill has turned a half-turn. This angle is twice as much as the quarter-turn.*

▶ The skater has turned one whole turn. This is twice as much as the half-turn, and four times as much as the quarter-turn.

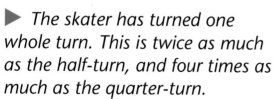

angle

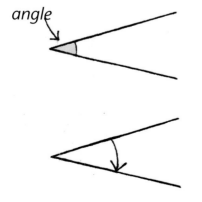

◀ *When two lines meet they make an angle. The angle is the amount of turn from facing along one line to facing along the other line.*

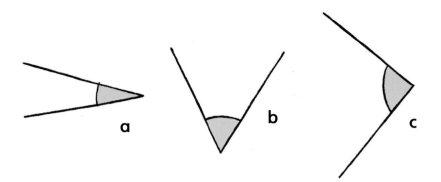

? Question

Which of these three angles is the smallest, and which the largest?

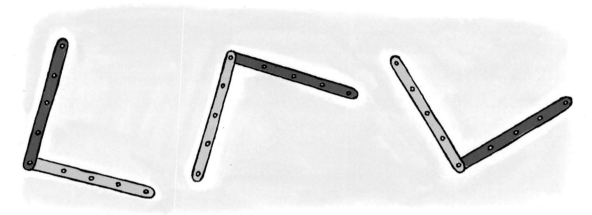

▲ *These three angles are all the same size. They are all quarter-turns. Quarter-turns are called **right-angles**.*

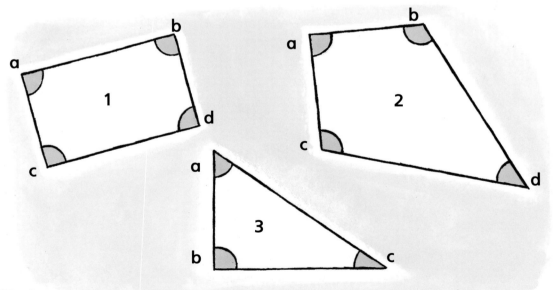

? Question

Which of the angles in these shapes are right-angles?

Types of angle

Angles are measured using different units.

You can measure quarter-turns in right-angles.

1 quarter-turn = 1 **right-angle**

2 quarter-turns = 2 right-angles

3 quarter-turns = 3 right-angles

4 quarter-turns = 4 right-angles

Sometimes the angles you are measuring are in between these quarter-turns. To measure these you use **degrees** as units.

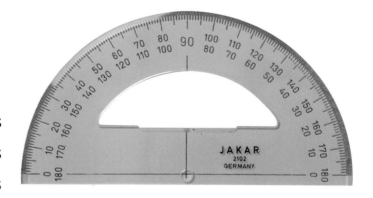

▲ There are 90 degrees in 1 right-angle.

The symbol ° means degrees, so we write 90 degrees as 90°.

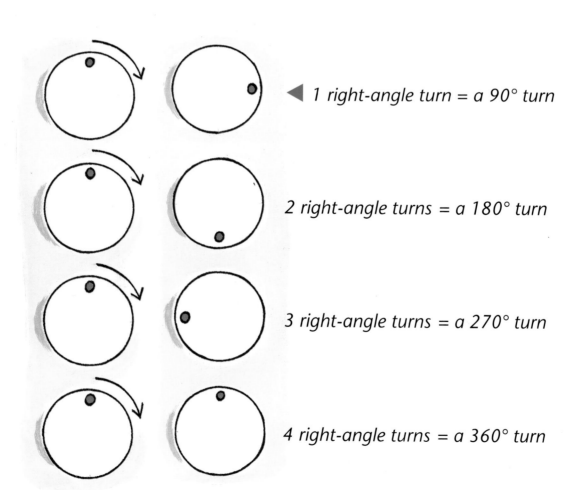

◄ *1 right-angle turn = a 90° turn*

2 right-angle turns = a 180° turn

3 right-angle turns = a 270° turn

4 right-angle turns = a 360° turn

What does it mean?

Angles which are:

- exactly 90° are called right-angles.

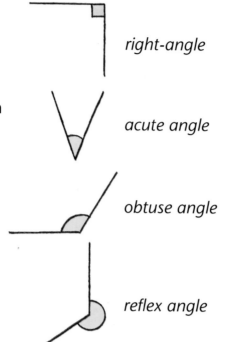

right-angle

- less than 1 right-angle, or less than 90°, are called **acute angles**.

acute angle

- between 1 and 2 right-angles, or between 90° and 180°, are called **obtuse angles**.

obtuse angle

- more than 2 right-angles, or more than 180°, are called **reflex angles**.

reflex angle

Use your head

Describe the angle turned through by the hand of each clock. Which are right-angles, acute angles, obtuse angles and which are reflex angles?

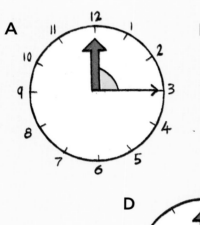

A

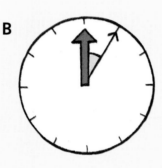

B

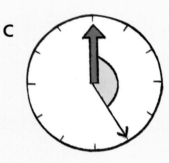

C

D

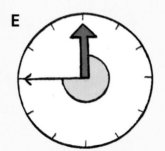

E

Polygons

A **polygon** is a flat (**two-dimensional**) shape which has straight sides.

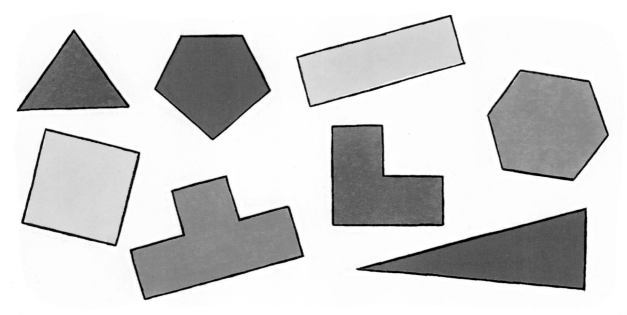

▲ *These are all examples of polygons.*

What does it mean?

Polygons have names, depending on how many sides they have.

All polygons have three or more straight sides, as shown in this table.

Their names are:

Sides	Name
3 sides	triangle
4 sides	quadrilateral
5 sides	pentagon
6 sides	hexagon
7 sides	heptagon
8 sides	octagon
9 sides	nonagon
10 sides	decagon

Fun to do

Draw your own set of polygons: one with 3 sides, one with 4 sides, and so on. Use a ruler to help you draw them. Write the correct names alongside each polygon.

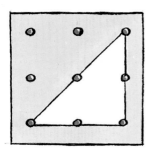 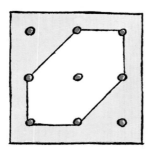 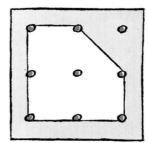 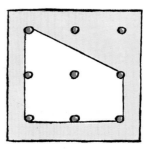

? Question

Can you name these polygons?

What does it mean?

A polygon which has all of its sides the same length, and all of its **angles** the same size is called a **regular polygon**. Polygons which are not regular are called **irregular polygons**.

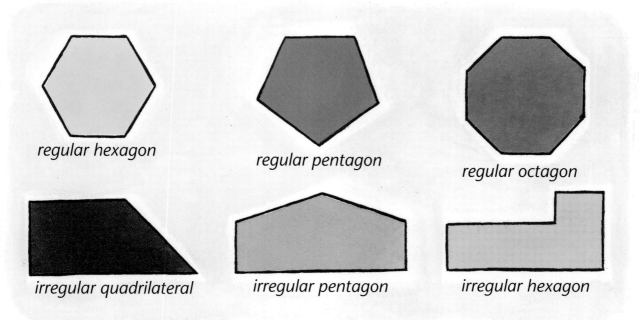

regular hexagon

regular pentagon

regular octagon

irregular quadrilateral

irregular pentagon

irregular hexagon

Some polygons have all of their sides the same length, but their angles are not the same size, so they are irregular.

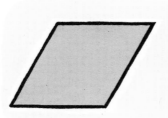 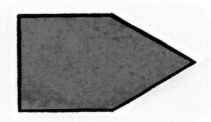

Triangles

A **triangle** is a 3-sided **polygon**. If an object is shaped like a triangle, then you can describe it as triangular.

There are many different triangular shapes all around us.

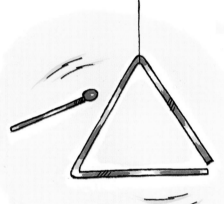

? Question

How many triangular-shaped surfaces can you spot here?

◀ *This musical instrument is called a **triangle**.*

What does it mean?

Different types of triangle have different names.

If all three sides of a triangle have different lengths, it is a **scalene triangle**.

If two of the sides of a triangle are the same length, it is an **isosceles triangle**. Triangles which are isosceles also have two equal **angles**.

◀ *All the sides of this triangle are different lengths.*

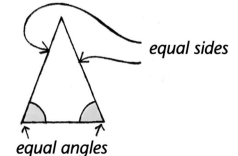

equal sides

equal angles

12

? **Question**
The tops of roofs are sometimes triangular-shaped. Can you see the isosceles triangles here?

What does it mean?

If all three sides of a triangle are the same length, it is an **equilateral triangle**.

An equilateral triangle not only has all of its sides the same length, but also its three angles are the same size. They are all 60°. Therefore it is a **regular polygon**. An equilateral triangle is a regular 3-sided polygon.

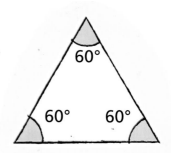

▶ *These road signs are very nearly shaped like equilateral triangles; the vertices are slightly rounded instead of being pointed.*

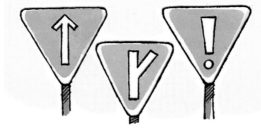

Fun to do

Make an equilateral triangle from a paper circle. First cut out a paper circle, and mark its centre. Fold from any point to the centre to make one side of the triangle. Fold to the centre again, from one end of the first side. Fold the last part to complete the equilateral triangle.

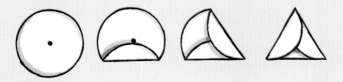

In some triangles, one of the angles is a **right-angle** (it is 90°). These triangles are called **right-angled triangles**. A right-angled triangle is a triangle which has one right-angle.

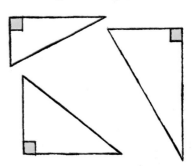

13

Lines

Parallel lines are straight lines or **curved** lines which are always the same distance apart. No matter how far you continue the lines, they will never meet.

▲ *Musical notes are written on or between parallel lines.*

▲ *The lanes on the running track are marked with parallel lines.*

What does it mean?

Perpendicular lines are straight lines which meet at right-angles.

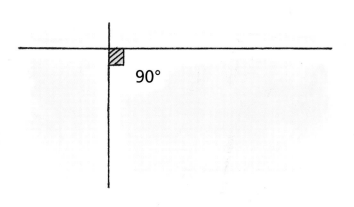

90°

▶ *These two lines are perpendicular. They meet at an angle of 90°.*

 Use your head

Which of the parts of the gate are parallel and which are perpendicular?

What does it mean?

The horizon is an imaginary line where the land or sea appear to meet the sky in the far distance.

Straight lines which go straight across the page from left to right are called **horizontal lines** (if you hold the book straight!). Horizontal lines get their name from horizon, because they are parallel to the horizon.

Straight lines which go straight up and down the page are called **vertical lines**. Vertical lines are perpendicular to horizontal lines.

◀ *We stand vertically, and lie down horizontally.*

▲ *Squared paper is drawn with horizontal and vertical lines. The horizontal lines are parallel to each other. The vertical lines are parallel to each other. Each vertical line is perpendicular to each horizontal line.*

Play the Noughts and Crosses game

This is a game for two players. Start by drawing two parallel lines, then another two which are perpendicular to these. One player is 'Nought' the other 'Cross'. Take turns to draw your symbol on the board. The winner is the first to make a straight line of three of their own symbol.

Quadrilaterals

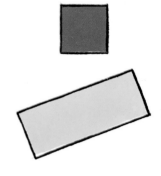

A **quadrilateral** is a 4-sided **polygon**. The most common examples of quadrilaterals are **squares** and **rectangles**.

A square is a special quadrilateral, because it is a **regular polygon**. It has four equal **sides**, and four equal **angles**. Its angles are all **right-angles** or 90°. It has two pairs of parallel sides.

▶ *Squares are everywhere. Squares and rectangles are probably the most common shapes.*

What does it mean?

A rectangle has similar properties to the square, except that most rectangles have two longer sides and two shorter sides. The longer sides are parallel to each other, and the shorter sides are also parallel to each other. Like the square, all of its angles are the same: 90°.

Objects or parts of objects which are shaped like a rectangle are described as rectangular.

? Question

Rectangles are all around us. Where can you see rectangles in this picture?

16

► A **parallelogram** is a different quadrilateral. It is like a squashed rectangle. When it is squashed, the angles change size, and are no longer right-angles. It is called a parallelogram because it still has two pairs of parallel sides.

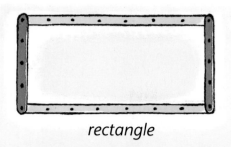

rectangle

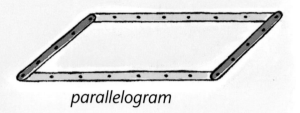

parallelogram

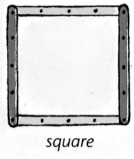

square

◄ A **rhombus** is like a squashed square. It is the same as a parallelogram, except that all its sides are the same length.

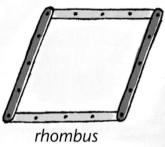

rhombus

A rectangle, a square, a parallelogram and a rhombus are all quadrilaterals which have two pairs of parallel sides.

► This quadrilateral has only one pair of parallel sides. It is called a **trapezium.**

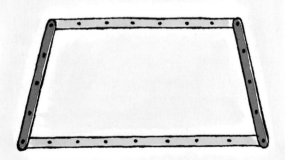

Solid shapes

These shapes have length, width, and thickness. They have three dimensions, and are called **three-dimensional shapes**. They may be solid or hollow.

For short, we sometimes say 3-D shape for three-dimensional shape.

A corner of a three-dimensional shape is called a **vertex** – the same name as the corner of a two-dimensional shape. The different shapes which make the outside of the shape or the surface of the shape are called **faces**. The sharp line where two faces meet is called an **edge**.

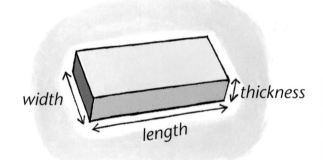

width

thickness

length

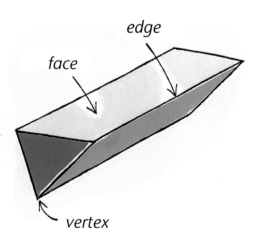

edge

face

vertex

This triangular **prism** has five faces. Some you can see and some are hidden.

Three of its faces are **rectangles** and two are **triangles**. You can say that it has three rectangular faces and two triangular faces.

? Questions

How many edges does it have?
How many vertices?
How many faces can you see, and how many are hidden?

◀ *These are all three-dimensional shapes.*

Some of the shapes have faces which are flat, and some have faces which are **curved**. Some have both flat and curved faces.

? Questions

Can you spot the shapes which have only a curved face? How many are there? How many have flat faces only? How many have both flat and curved faces?

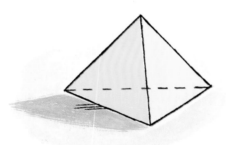

◀ *The faces of this shape are all **polygons**. A three-dimensional shape whose faces are all polygons is called a **polyhedron**. If the shape is made from a set of identical **regular polygons**, then the shape is called a regular polyhedron.*

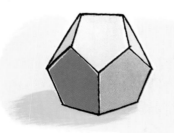

◀ *This polyhedron is made from regular pentagons, so it is a regular polyhedron.*

Cubes and cuboids

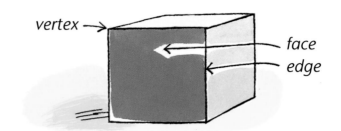

vertex →

face
edge

? **Question**

Can you count the **faces**, **vertices** and **edges** of this shape?

A **cube** is a common **three-dimensional shape**. It has 6 faces, each the same sized **square**. It has 8 vertices and 12 edges. Opposite faces are **parallel** to each other.

If a shape is shaped like a cube, you can describe it as cubic.

What does it mean?

A **cuboid** is a box shape. It has 6 faces, the same as a cube. It has 8 vertices, the same as a cube. Its faces, however, are a mixture of squares and **rectangles**.

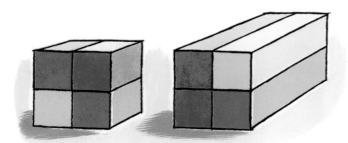

Cubes and cuboids are very common. One reason is that they pack together without leaving any gaps. You say that shapes which do this **tessellate**.

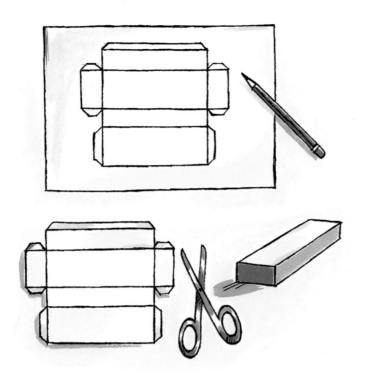

You can make three-dimensional shapes from card. You start by drawing an outline on the card, including the tabs which help hold it together. Cut out the outline. Score the lines using a ruler and ball-point pen to help them fold, glue the tabs and stick the shape together.

The outline drawn on the card is called a **net**. This is a net of a cuboid.

Use your head

There are many different nets of a cube. Some of these drawings are nets, and can build a cube, and some can not. Can you work out which are nets of a cube and which are not?

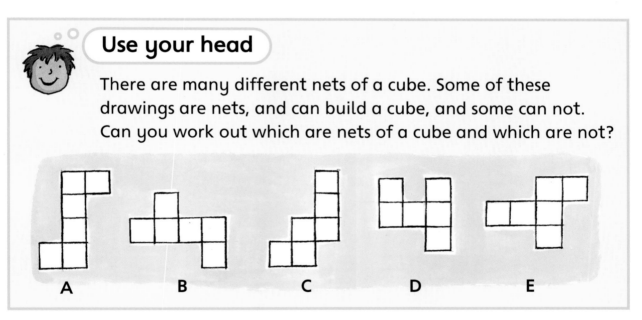

A   B   C   D   E

Fun to do

Make a dice. Start by drawing the net of a cube with tabs, on card. Next draw spots on the six faces: one to six. Score the lines, fold along them and stick the tabs to make the dice. Play a game with the dice.

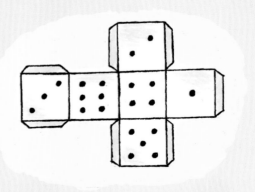

Pyramids, cones and spheres

This shape is called a **pyramid**. It has a bottom **face**, or base, on which it stands, and side faces which meet at a point, the peak or apex of the pyramid.

The side faces are all **triangles**. The bottom face or base can be different shapes. If it is a triangle, then the pyramid is called a triangular-based pyramid. If the base is **square**, then the pyramid is called a square-based pyramid.

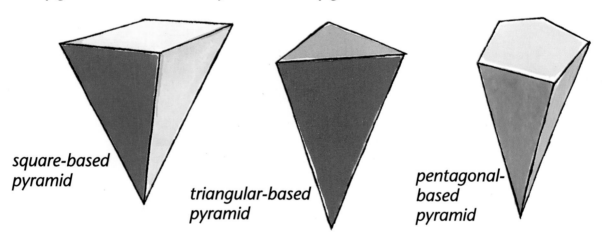

square-based pyramid

triangular-based pyramid

pentagonal-based pyramid

▶ *The ancient Egyptians created pyramid-shaped buildings which they used as tombs, and which still stand today. We call them the Egyptian pyramids.*

What does it mean?

A **cone** is like a pyramid which has a circular base. It has one curved face and one circular face. Many cones we see are hollow rather than solid. Traffic cones and ice-cream cones are very nearly perfect cones, except that their peaks are slightly rounded instead of perfectly pointed.

If an object is shaped like a cone, we describe it as conical.

Fun to do

Make a cone from a paper circle. Draw a straight line from the outside to the centre, then cut along it. Curl the paper into a cone, then stick it together with sticky tape.

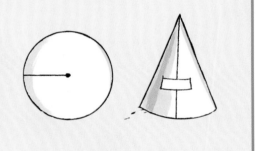

What does it mean?

This ball-shape is very common. It is called a **sphere**. It has one perfectly rounded face, with no **vertices**, and no **edges**.

An object which is shaped like a sphere is described as spherical.

What does it mean?

When you cut a sphere into two identical halves, each piece is half a sphere. This shape is called a **hemisphere**.

Prisms and cylinders

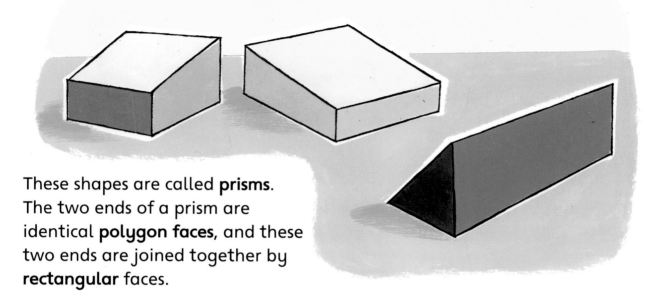

These shapes are called **prisms**. The two ends of a prism are identical **polygon faces**, and these two ends are joined together by **rectangular** faces.

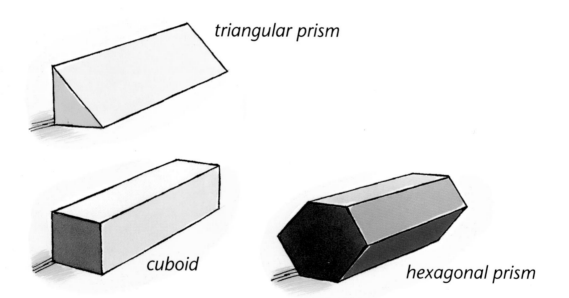

triangular prism

cuboid

hexagonal prism

▲ *These are different shaped prisms. The shape of the end face describes the prism. If the end face is a **triangle**, the prism is described as a triangular prism. If the end face is a hexagon, the prism is a hexagonal prism.*

*Notice that a prism whose end face is a **square** or **rectangle** is a simple box shape, and therefore is more commonly called a **cuboid**.*

These are different **nets** for prisms. Can you describe the type of prism each will make?

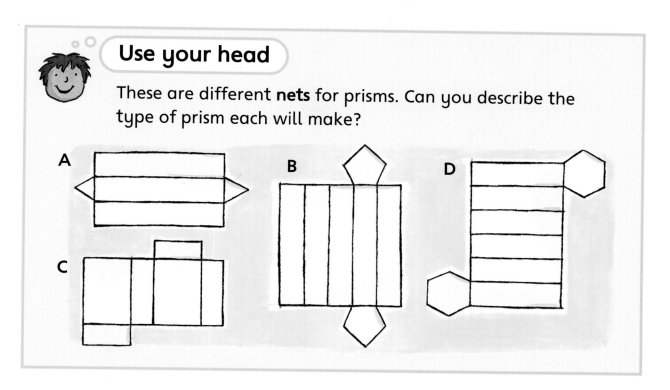

A

B

C

D

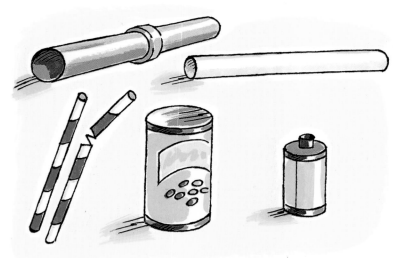

◀ These shapes are called **cylinders**. They are prisms with circular end-faces. A cylinder has two faces which are circles, and one **curved** face to hold them together.

If an object is a cylinder shape, it is described as cylindrical.

Fun to do

Make a paper cylinder. Roll a sheet of paper into a cylinder, and use two pieces of sticky tape to seal the join. Use different sized sheets of paper to make different shaped cylinders.

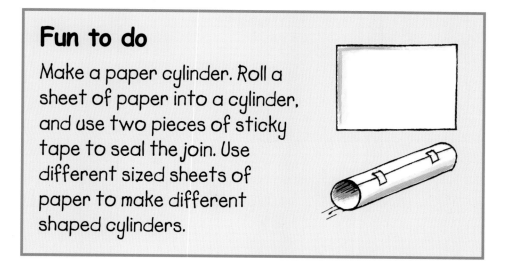

Coordinates

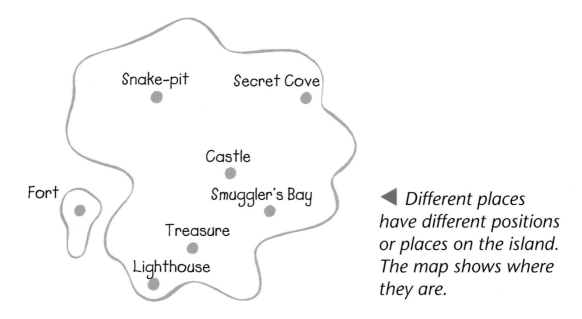

◀ *Different places have different positions or places on the island. The map shows where they are.*

Where is the Castle?
Where is the Lighthouse?
It is not easy to describe the positions of these places.

▶ *This is a square grid made from horizontal and vertical lines. The lines are numbered from 0 to 9. Make a square grid like this. If you draw the map on your square grid, the numbered lines will help you to describe where the different places are.*

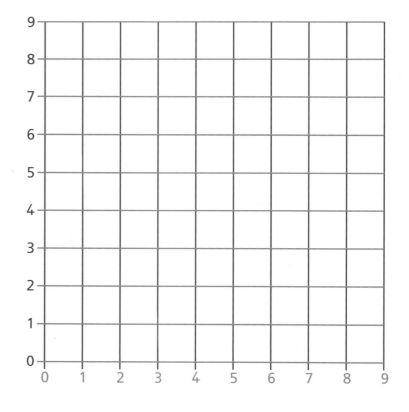

What does it mean?

The grid is called a **coordinate grid**.
It has a **horizontal** axis, going across the bottom (red),
and a **vertical** axis, going up the left (blue).

Search for the Treasure. It lies where two lines meet:

- line number 4 on the horizontal axis. 4 is called its horizontal coordinate.
- line number 2 on the vertical axis. 2 is called its vertical coordinate.

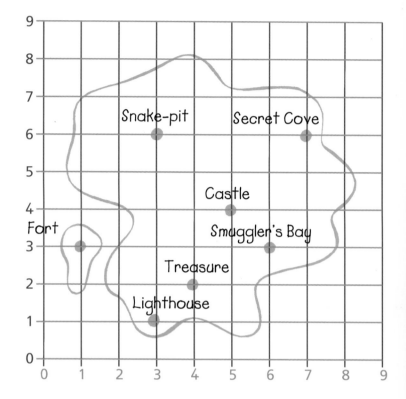

The Treasure has a horizontal coordinate of 4, and a vertical coordinate of 2.

You describe its position by these two numbers, always saying the horizontal number first, then the vertical number.

The Treasure has coordinates (4, 2), 'four-two'.

The Snake-pit has a first coordinate of 3, and a second coordinate of 6.
It is at the point (3, 6).

- -

Play the coordinate game

Draw a coordinate grid labelled from 1 to 6 on each axis. Use two dice, one red (for the horizontal coordinate) and the other blue (for the vertical coordinate). Take turns to throw both dice and mark the matching point on the grid in your own colour. The winner is the first to mark three points in any straight line.

Use your head

Describe the position of the Fort. Now describe the position of the Castle.

What will you find at these places:
(7, 6), (6, 3)?

Direction

◄ *From where you are standing, can you point in the direction of:*

- *your school*
- *your friend's house*
- *the shops*
- *France?*

What does it mean?

To help us describe the directions of places to others, we use four main directions: north, south, east and west.

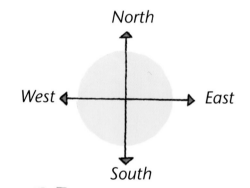

▶ *North and south are opposite directions. West and east are opposite directions.*

What does it mean?

A compass is an instrument for measuring direction. If you hold the compass horizontally it shows you where the four main directions are.

▶ *Since some directions may not be exactly north, south, east or west, there are four other 'in-between' directions. Half-way between north and east, for example, is described as north-east.*

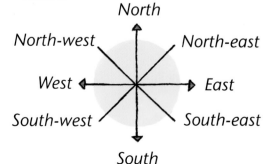

What does it mean?

To describe directions, you use the first letters for shorthand:

N stands for north   **S**: south

E: east   **W**: west

NE stands for north-east   **NW**: north-west

SE: south-east   **SW**: south-west

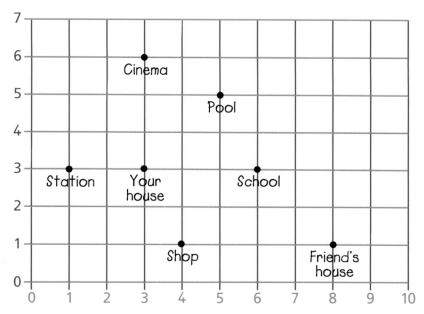

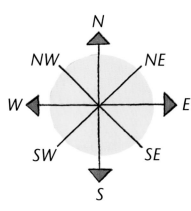

▲ *The map shows the position of different places. The directions are shown beside the map.*

If you are standing at 'your house', the cinema is in the direction north, the school is east, the pool is north-east.

If you are standing at the cinema, your house is south.

Use your head

Can you describe these directions:

- your house from the school?
- the school from the shop?
- the school from the station?
- your friend's house from the school?

Glossary

acute angle	an angle which measures less than one right-angle
angle	an amount of turn measured in degrees
cone	3-D shape with a pointed vertex and a circular base
coordinate grid	grid to help find positions of objects
coordinates	a pair of numbers which describe the position of a point on a coordinate grid
cube	cuboid with identical square faces
cuboid	3-D shape which has six rectangular faces
curved	not straight
cylinder	3-D shape with circular ends of equal size
degree	small unit for measuring an angle
edge	where two faces of a 3-D shape meet
equilateral triangle	triangle with all sides the same length
face	one of the flat or curved surfaces of a 3-D shape
hemisphere	half a sphere
horizontal line	a straight line from left to right on paper which is held straight; a line parallel to the horizon
irregular polygon	polygon in which the sides or angles are not equal
isosceles triangle	triangle with two equal sides
net	a 2-D drawing which we can cut out to make a 3-D shape
obtuse angle	an angle which measures between one and two right-angles
parallel lines	lines which stay the same distance apart along their whole length
parallelogram	a quadrilateral with two pairs of parallel sides
perpendicular lines	straight lines which meet at right-angles
polygon	2-D shape with straight sides
polyhedron	3-D shape with faces that are polygons

prism	3-D shape that has the same cross-section all along its length
pyramid	3-D shape with a polygon for its base and triangular faces that meet at one vertex
quadrilateral	2-D shape with four straight sides
rectangle	a quadrilateral with four right-angles
reflex angle	an angle which measures more than two right-angles
regular polygon	a polygon with all its sides and angles equal
rhombus	a parallelogram with equal sides
right-angle	a quarter-turn
right-angled triangle	a triangle with one right-angle
scalene triangle	a triangle with all its sides of different lengths and all its angles of different sizes
side	the edge of a 2-D shape
sphere	perfectly round 3-D shape like a ball
square	rectangle with four equal sides
surface	the top or outside of an object or shape
tessellate	shapes tessellate if they fit snugly together without leaving gaps
two-dimensional shape	flat shape, drawn on paper. It has length and width, but no thickness.
trapezium	a quadrilateral with one pair of parallel sides
triangle	2-D shape with three straight sides and three angles
three-dimensional shape	solid or hollow shape. It has length, width and thickness.
vertex	corner of a 2-D or a 3-D shape; the plural (the word for more than one) is vertices
vertical line	a straight line drawn from top to bottom, at right-angles to a horizontal line

Answers

Page 5
Question
A: square: 4 sides, 4 vertices
B, I: triangle: 3 sides, 3 vertices
C, J: rhombus: 4 sides, 4 vertices
D, E, G: hexagon: 6 sides, 6 vertices
F: rectangle: 4 sides, 4 vertices
H: circle: 1 side, 0 vertices
Use your head
straight: 5
curved: 3
straight and curved: 3

Page 7
Question
a is smallest
c is largest
Question
1a, 1b, 1c, 1d, 2a, 3b are right-angles

Page 9
Use your head
A: 1 right-angle
B: acute angle
C: obtuse angle
D: reflex angle
E: 3 right-angles = reflex angle

Page 11
Question
triangle, hexagon, pentagon, quadrilateral (trapezium)

Page 12
Question 7

Page 13
Question
the roofs are made up of isosceles triangles

Page 14
Use your head
parallels: the 5 horizontal bars, the 2 vertical bars
perpendicular: each horizontal bar to each vertical post

Page 16
Question
the roof and wall of the building; the door; the paving stones on patio

Page 18
Question
9 edges, 6 vertices
3 faces seen, 2 faces hidden

Page 19
Question
a curved face only: 1
flat faces only: 4
both flat and curved faces: 3

Page 20
Question
6 faces, 8 vertices, 12 edges

Page 21
Use your head
nets of cube: A, B, E
not nets of cube: C, D

Page 25
Use your head
A: triangular prism
B: pentagonal prism
C: cuboid
D: hexagonal prism

Page 27
Use your head
Fort: (1, 3)
Castle: (5, 4)
(7, 6): Secret Cove
(6, 3): Smuggler's Bay

Page 29
Use your head
west; north-east; east; south-east

Index